Dwarf and
Slow-growing Conifers

A Wisley Handbook

Dwarf and Slow-growing Conifers

JOHN BOND and LYN RANDALL

Cassell

The Royal Horticultural Society

THE ROYAL HORTICULTURAL SOCIETY

Cassell Educational Limited
Villiers House, 41/47 Strand
London WC2N 5JE
for the Royal Horticultural Society

First published 1987
Reprinted 1988
Second edition 1993

British Library Cataloguing in Publication Data
A catalogue record for this book is available from the British Library

ISBN 0–304–32065–X

Line drawings by Sue Wickison

Photographs by Photos Horticultural and Lyn Randall

Phototypesetting by RGM Associates, Southport
Printed in Hong Kong by Wing King Tong Co. Ltd.

Cover: A conifer and heather garden, an excellent example
of contrast in form and colour.
Back cover: A fine specimen of *Juniper horizontalis* 'Glauca'
with one-year ground cover.
p.1: A fine selection of some of the best dwarf conifers.
p.2: This conifer garden is set in crazy paving for low
maintenance.
Photographs by Photos Horticultural

Contents

The popular *Chamaecyparis pisifera* 'Boulevard', an example of a slow-growing conifer which may eventually become too large (see p. 30)

Introduction

Ask the question 'What is your opinion of dwarf conifers?' among your circle of gardening friends and you will very likely receive one of the following answers: 'Weird, abnormal, certainly not for me'; 'Wonderful, exciting, an absorbing group of plants'; or, most frequently, 'But they never stay dwarf, do they?'

There is a great deal of truth in this last reply, for there are very few truly dwarf conifers, that is those attaining an ultimate height and spread of 2 by 2 feet (60 × 60 cm). There are, however, many other fine conifers which, although they will eventually reach a height of 4 to 6 feet (1.2–1.8 m) and a similar spread, will achieve these dimensions only after very many years. (Rates of growth vary according to the species and environment and it is not possible to be more precise.) It is for this reason that the title *Dwarf and Slow-growing Conifers*, rather than *Dwarf Conifers*, has been chosen for this book.

The statement 'Weird, abnormal, etc.' is another fairly common comment and again it contains some truth. A few dwarf conifers do have a strange appearance, but these are a very small minority compared to the many normal forms which can be obtained.

The third answer, in favour of dwarf conifers, is the most usual reaction. There is a wealth of first-rate plants available and these can and do provide a growing number of gardeners with an absorbing hobby. In fact, be warned; if you become 'hooked' on dwarf conifers, you are in danger of having your lives, and your gardens, dominated by them.

Dwarf conifers are undoubtedly plants for today, with gardens continually shrinking in size. Great care should be taken in planting these small areas where space is at a premium and scale all important, paying particular attention to the ultimate size of the plants chosen.

It should be made clear to all readers that this book is concerned with conifers which remain naturally dwarf or slow-growing, without any artificial aid such as root pruning or root restriction in small containers. (This form of cultivation is called bonsai and is dealt with adequately in many books, including an excellent volume in this series.)

One last reminder—conifers provide us with the best of evergreens and are more than capable of holding the stage throughout the year.

Uses in the Garden

The landscape value of conifers is in no doubt. Being mostly ever-green, they add great strength of form, shelter and frequently privacy to the garden. This is particularly obvious if the garden contains a strong element of deciduous trees and shrubs. Conifers have a similar role to play, on a much larger scale, in the country-side. Because Britain is poorly endowed with native conifers—just three species, only one of which is a respec-table tree—we rely heavily on foreign introductions for forestry and general landscape purposes. Many people wish that these exotics had not been so extensively planted, particularly the vast masses of Sitka spruce which have produced such a boring land-scape in parts of the country. There is certainly a lesson for the gardener to learn from this—think very carefully about the plac-ing of your conifers and make sure that every one of them has a part in the overall design.

We are fortunate in having a range of highly ornamental species and forms of conifers, suitable for gardens of all sizes. In the 25-acre garden, for example, trees with an ultimate height of 50 to 100 feet (15–30 m) can be used safely and for the one-acre garden there are many which will fairly slowly attain 25 feet (7 m). There is no reason why the great variety of smaller conifers should not also be used in these larger gardens. However, it is in the small garden so common today that dwarf and slower-growing conifers come into their own and provide the same effect, scaled down, as their larger allies.

As already pointed out, it is very important to consider the ultimate height and spread of dwarf conifers when selecting them for specific purposes. So much of their garden value is in the form and outline, which will be completely lost if the plants are crowded or allowed to grow into one another. Even worse, branches may die and leave unsightly gaps.

One of the major concerns of modern gardeners is time and, quite understandably, slow-growing plants have little to recom-mend them when an instant garden is required. This is a particular problem in the case of dwarf conifers, since mature specimens are rarely offered by nurseries and are consequently very expensive. There is, however, a solution.

The reader will remember that we are considering true dwarf conifers with an ultimate height and spread of 2 by 2 feet (60 × 60 cm) and slow-growing forms which will eventually reach

6 by 6 feet (1.8 × 1.8 m). My suggestion is to plant some temporarily, to fill the space until the permanent plants have grown. For example, forms with an ultimate size of 4 feet (1.2 m) are planted where 2 feet (60 cm) will be required, 6 feet (1.8 m) for 4 feet (1.2 m) and 8 to 10 feet (2.4–3 m) for 6 feet (1.8 m). These 'fillers' or short-term plants are then removed when the long-term plants, already planted in their correct sites, have grown sufficiently large to create the desired effect. This plan calls for a well researched planting scheme and careful selection of both the short- and long-term plants—colour, form and ultimate size being most important. It also demands a certain toughness from the gardener when the time for removal arrives, for we are often too tender-hearted about disposing of trees and shrubs from our gardens. The short-term plants, if in good condition, could be transplanted to other areas of the garden.

The plan outlined above is probably most applicable in a fairly wide border, with room for the tallest plants at the back and the smallest at the front. Welcome irregularity can be achieved by placing a few slightly larger specimens at the front and, of course, by using some spreading forms. Shape and colour will play an important part in the overall design and you may want to introduce a few deciduous plants for contrast, which could include some with fine foliage, such as the forms of Acer palmatum 'Dissectum', and even roses where space allows. These would ease the heavy, somewhat stodgy general appearance of the conifers and would also provide interest and colour during the months when conifers are in a less decorative phase.

The island bed offers a most attractive setting for dwarf conifers and arguably the greatest challenge, for it must achieve perfection on all four sides. Again, contrasting plants can be used with the conifers—dwarf bulbs, thymes, a collection of campanulas, dwarf heathers—the range of suitable plants is endless. A few well chosen and carefully placed pieces of stone might add to the effect. Another idea is to associate a fine block of stone or rock with a single conifer on a lawn, to provide an eye-catching feature. It should be emphasized that there are numerous dwarf and slow-growing conifers for a border or island bed of any size and that an area of a few square feet or considerably larger will be equally exciting to plant.

Dwarf conifers are invariably regarded as ideal for the rock garden, but only certain kinds are appropriate. It is better to choose those of prostrate or irregular and windswept appearance, and then only if they are very slow to develop, and to avoid those of regular and perfect outline—unless you want to create a setting for gnomes!

Heathers associate particularly well with dwarf conifers to provide
interest throughout the year

The heather garden offers much more scope, particularly for
conifers of uneven shape like the dwarf pines. Although some
people may find the association somewhat overdone for their
taste, there is no doubt that a selection of heathers to flower all the
year round, together with a carefully chosen range of conifers,
will produce a very effective garden of reasonably low maintenance and continuous interest. Many conifers are especially
valuable in winter, when they take on beautiful colours of gold,
deeper gold or bronze and attractive hues of brown and purple.

Much has been written in recent times in praise of ground
cover. Providing the soil is first cleared of perennial weeds,

Juniperus communis 'Hornibrookii' is well known and an ideal plant
for ground cover (see p. 36)

labour can be greatly reduced by the close planting of ground
cover, which will prevent further germination and development
of weeds (see also the Wisley Handbook, *Ground Cover Plants*).
Conifers, particularly the dense prostrate junipers, are excellent
for this purpose, but will take at least two or three years to
become fully effective. Such plants are also extremely useful for
clothing and stabilizing steep banks and similar difficult sites.

So far, we have discussed the use of dwarf and slow-growing
conifers in informal settings. There are many other extremely
good conifers of regular, near perfect outline which lend themselves to formal situations—the two sentinels at the front door or
gate, for instance, which are always popular. While very few
dwarf conifers make good hedges, a large number of formal
outline are suitable for low partitions or screens, which can be
desirable features in their own right and are ideal for surrounding
a formal or kitchen garden. Many dwarf conifers are also reliable
in large containers. These should not be too small, for a larger
amount of soil will ensure a longer life for the plant in this somewhat artificial form of gardening.

11

Origins

The recent convert to dwarf conifers may well expect that they all come from mountainous areas and are normally dwarf in the wild. This is true of a few species, for instance *Pinus mugo* from the European Alps, *P. pumila* from Japan and *Juniperus horizontalis* from the mountains of north eastern America, which have given us numerous good dwarf forms. However, most dwarf selections have originated quite differently. These three species are reliable dwarf conifers; other natives of high mountains are less trustworthy and may produce seedlings whose dwarfing has been caused by the harsh climatic conditions (which may also occur in severe maritime exposure). If these are lifted and grown in more favourable garden conditions, they rapidly assume a normal tall stature.

So much for dwarf conifers in the wild; a more lucrative source of true dwarf forms is the nurseryman's seed bed. When thousands of seeds are sown, there is often considerable variation among the resulting seedlings, which can lead to dramatic differences in foliage, form, colour and speed of development. Similar changes can also occur among naturally regenerated seedlings and the keen enthusiast should watch out for these when walking through the forest. Not all species of conifer are equally free in producing variations of offspring. *Chamaecyparis lawsoniana* is one of the most prolific and a batch of its seedlings is likely to produce a great range of coloured and slower-growing forms.

Branch sporting, a further source of new forms including dwarf ones, is of great interest. Sports are genetically sound and distinct changes in colour or growth which occur on normal branches. When these new growths are sufficiently large, propagating material is removed and, if the resulting plants are considered distinct and worthy of garden space, a stock of new plants will be built up by the nurseryman.

The final source of dwarf conifers is perhaps the most exciting and is responsible for many of the finest forms. A number of conifers, in particular the pines, spruces and silver firs, frequently develop 'witches' brooms', which are congested, tight and gnarled bundles of small, but otherwise healthy, growths attached to normal branches. These brooms are thought to be the result of parasitic or some other pathological interference. If propagation material is removed and grafted, it will provide first-class new

A conifer garden showing an effective contrast of shapes and colours

plants, which usually remain dwarf. Of great interest is the fact that these brooms or the resulting propagations often produce diminutive cones, complete with small seeds. If these seeds are sown, many will produce new and most desirable dwarf conifers.

We would like to make a plea at this stage to anyone involved in raising new dwarf conifers. Please assess the selected plant very thoroughly before naming and releasing stock to our gardens, for we already have a wealth of plants available and anything new must be distinct and, above all, reliable and worthwhile.

JUVENILE AND ADULT FOLIAGE

All seed-raised conifers begin life with leaves of a distinctly heather-like appearance, known as juvenile foliage, which is quite different from the adult foliage developed by the plant as it matures. This juvenile foliage is occasionally held by the plant throughout its life and remains fixed when propagated vegetatively. There are many desirable dwarf conifers of this kind.

The junipers are a well known example of a genus where both types of foliage are present. Some species, like *J. communis*, retain the juvenile leaves permanently; others, such as *J. virginiana*, produce juvenile and adult leaves together. Foliage intermediate between the juvenile and adult states may also be found, as in the case of the Plumosa group of *Chamaecyparis pisifera*.

13

— Cultivation and Propagation —

SUITABLE CONDITIONS

Conifers will thrive in any good soil, although many are tolerant of very poor soil conditions, including the poorest peaty acid soils. The exception is soil with a high lime content or thin soil over chalk where there are serious limitations. However, we are saved by two genera, the junipers and the yews, which will succeed in limy conditions, and luckily both contain many good and useful dwarf forms. Apart from the spruces and a few others, conifers will not accept waterlogged soil.

Poor soil is not a disadvantage; in fact, it may well be advantageous, because dwarf conifers will grow and develop slowly in such a soil and will therefore assume more desirable and attractive characteristics. But poor soils are frequently dry soils and watering may be necessary to ensure that conifers do not become too dry, particularly when newly planted. Once established, however, plants should not require watering if a good mulch is applied regularly.

Mulching not only conserves moisture, but helps to restrict weed growth and make the task of weeding less irksome, for any weeds that do grow may be easily removed. It also gives an attractive finish to the surface and, if evenly applied, it will improve the appearance of all permanent plantings. The first choice of mulching material should be leafmould, either from hardwood trees such as oak or beech, or from softwood trees like pine, the latter being particularly suitable since it inevitably contains small cones and freshly fallen needles which blend well with dwarf conifers. Other sources of mulch are shredded bark, wood chips and peat, although this should only be used as a last resort in view of its cost. The mulch is best applied in winter, to a depth of 2 or 3 inches (5–8 cm), when the soil is wet.

Organic and inorganic fertilizers should not be necessary and, if used at all, should be used only sparingly. Heavy feeding will result in fast uncharacteristic growth.

Dwarf conifers, with their compact, stocky form, are generally wind-resistant, but planting in frost pockets should be avoided. Frosts in late spring can be especially troublesome, damaging the new soft young shoots. In a severe winter, the tight close growth of certain dwarf conifers holds large quantities of water which, when frozen hard, results in whole branchlets being killed, thus

'Rigid Dwarf', like many of the very dwarf forms of *Chamaecyparis obtusa*, needs winter protection (see p. 27)

ruining the entire plant. Many of those susceptible, particularly the diminutive forms of *Chamaecyparis obtusa* and *C. pisifera*, are safer in an alpine house; alternatively, they may be protected by a pane of glass held above the plant on four sticks.

Heavy snowfall can be another problem, especially with conifers of upright growth which are forced open by the weight of the snow. A sharp knock with a broom handle should dislodge the snow and restore the branches to their natural shape.

Very few conifers are able to tolerate shade, the yews being the only exception, and this particularly applies to dwarf conifers. In fact, full exposure to light is essential to get the finest shape and colour from dwarf conifers.

CHOOSING AND PLANTING

Almost all dwarf conifers offered for sale today are grown in containers and if well developed plants are bought, there should be no difficulty in establishing them at any time of year. The best period is from October to April, when the weather is normally moister and cooler and the plants are dormant. However, planting should never be done if the soil is frozen, as the roots could be damaged.

15

There is a tendency with container-grown plants for the roots to encircle the base of the container. These roots should be carefully unravelled before being spread out around the area of the planting hole. Make sure that the hole is large enough to take the whole root system without crowding and place the plant in the ground only fractionally deeper than it was in the container. Then replace the soil and firm it well around the plant. The whole planting operation should be performed with great care and thoroughness, for our chosen dwarf conifers are likely to remain in the garden for many years.

If plants from the open ground (as opposed to container-grown) are acquired, perhaps from friends or transplanted from your own garden, they will need special attention in the first year after planting, for even if the plant is lifted with a good ball of soil, some roots are bound to have been damaged. Watering in dry weather will be necessary and a screen of hessian shading to provide shelter from sun and wind will help the new plant to become established. If the plant is large and perhaps has only a small root ball, it should be supported with a stake during the first year or two to reduce stress from the wind.

When selecting plants from the nursery, look for ones which are a good shape, without any unsightly holes, bare stems or dead twigs or branches. They should appear healthy and have a good colour, keeping in mind the great variation in colour and the fact that many conifers change colour when slightly starved in containers or during the winter months.

Whenever possible, choose plants on their own roots rather than grafted plants. The latter tend to be much more vigorous and may lose important characteristics because of the fast-growing species which are used as rootstocks. Most dwarf forms of *Chamaecyparis, Cryptomeria, Juniperus, Picea, Taxus* and *Thuja* are easily propagated by cuttings and should be generally available on their own roots. However, *Abies, Cedrus, Cupressus, Larix, Pinus* and *Pseudotsuga* are only very rarely offered on their own roots. These have to be grafted and will be more expensive in view of the greater expertise involved in their propagation. When selecting grafted plants, always look for a good clean union between scion and stock and ensure that there are no suckers arising from below the union.

PRUNING

The pruning of dwarf conifers is a controversial matter. Many experts recommend leaving the plants to take their own course, while others are in favour of judicious shaping and checking of

Dwarf conifers mingle well with alpines in a raised bed

the rank growth which unfortunately appears on some forms. If pruning is practised, it is very important not to spoil the general outline and character of the plant (a topiary-type specimen is the last thing that is wanted!).

The effects of poor soil and full exposure have already been referred to (see pp. 14 and 15). Root pruning may be used in the same way, to help slow down the rate of growth and maintain the true shape of the plant. This operation should be carried out in winter, by inserting a sharp spade to its full depth around the plant at the perimeter of the branches.

Conifers, in common with all evergreens, lose their leaves during the summer months. Many dwarf conifers hold this dead foliage among their twigs and branches which prevents light and air reaching the centre of the plant. This is particularly troublesome in the very tight-growing forms and will result in a considerable number of dead branchlets if the debris is not cleared away—a tedious but very necessary task.

PROPAGATION

Propagation of many conifers from cuttings is comparatively easy, although some can only be increased by grafting (see p. 16). Any rank strong growth at the top of the mother plant should be avoided when taking cuttings, for while this is often easier to root, it will produce plants with uncharacteristic loose growth. Short slow growth is the ideal material. Cuttings may be taken either with a heel (a piece of the main stem attached) or as firm tip growth between August and March, the optimum time being September to November, and are best inserted in a frame with bottom heat. Good results can also be obtained using a cold frame in August and September. More difficult genera, the dwarf spruces and dwarf tsugas for example, will respond more readily if placed under a mist system. A mixture of 50% peat and 50% sharp sand is the normal medium for rooting and a hormone rooting powder will improve the percentage of rooted cuttings. If a frame is used, it will be necessary to spray the cuttings with water twice daily in warm weather and to shade the frame on sunny days.

Grafting presents a greater challenge and certainly adds interest for the keen enthusiast. The task, however, calls for some skill and is outside the scope of this book. There are several specialist books on propagation which will provide all the necessary details, including *The Grafter's Handbook* by R.J. Garner (fifth edition, 1988, Cassell).

Opposite: outline shapes of dwarf conifers: 1 bun-shaped; 2 mound-shaped; 3 globose; 4 pyramidal; 5 conical; 6 columnar; 7 weeping; 8 ground-hugging; 9 prostrate; 10 semi-prostrate; 11 wide-spreading.

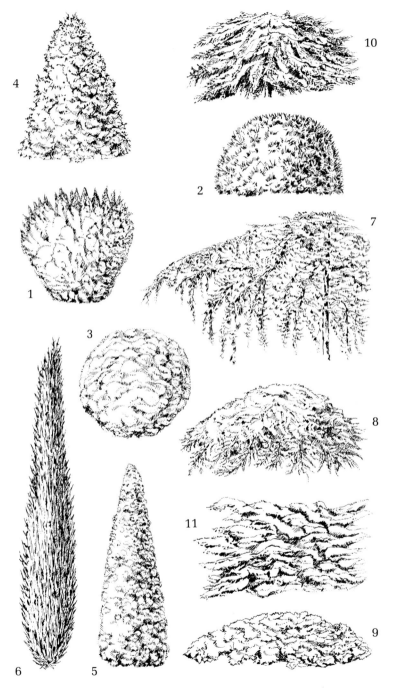

— Recommended Dwarf Conifers —

The following list is arranged in alphabetical order of genus and gives brief descriptions of some of the most worthwhile cultivars. It also includes rarer plants (indicated by an asterisk *), which are not normally available from general nurseries and garden centres, but may often be obtained from growers specializing in dwarf and slow-growing conifers.

Measurements refer to the expected height and width after ten years, unless otherwise stated. However, these are only approximate and will vary according to growing conditions.

Abies

The silver firs are some of the grandest and most beautiful trees to be seen in the wild and their native habitat extends through the northern hemisphere from North America to Europe and China. Some species have particularly attractive cones and others are strikingly colourful in spring when male and female 'flowers' appear. Regrettably, they do not lend themselves readily to producing dwarf forms, although there are a few good small and slow-growing varieties.

A. amabilis is the red silver fir from the foothills of western North America and has given rise to a superb horizontal form, 'Spreading Star'*. The silver-grey, needle-like leaves provide an attractive background for the bright red male cones in the spring. ($3\frac{1}{4} \times 5$–$6\frac{3}{4}$ ft; 1×1.5–2 m.)

A. balsamea, the balsam fir, is another North American native and is not tolerant of chalky soils. There are two very good dwarf forms.

'Hudsonia' has dark green foliage and forms a rounded compact bush. The needles are held semi-radially, leaving a distinct parting on the stems. It is hardy and trouble-free. ($1\frac{1}{2}$ ft; 50 cm.)

'Nana' is similar but, since the leaves are arranged all around the stems, it has a denser look.

A. cephalonica, a mountain species from Greece, is ideal for chalky soils. The only dwarf form, 'Meyer's Dwarf' (formerly called 'Nana'), is an attractive flat-topped plant. Very slow-growing and compact, it does not produce a leading shoot. ($3\frac{1}{4}$ ft; 1 m.)

A. *concolor*, the Colorado white fir, is a beautiful mountain species which has produced a fine dwarf called 'Compacta', often offered under the name 'Glauca Compacta'. It is of compact but irregular growth. ($3\frac{1}{4}$ ft; 1 m.)

'Pigglemee'* is a new dwarf cultivar which is worth searching for at specialist nurseries.

A. *koreana*, although not a dwarf, is included here for its slow growth and for its usefulness in the border or as a specimen plant in the larger garden. It originates from mountainous areas of Korea and has attractive foliage of glossy green with white undersides. However, the most notable feature is the blue cones, which are held upright on the branches and, unlike many other *Abies* species, produced at an early age. ($9\frac{3}{4}$ ft; 3 m; see p. 22.)

'Compact Dwarf' is very small with horizontally held branches, but unfortunately no cones. ($2\frac{1}{2}$ ft; 70 cm.)

'Prostrate Beauty' is a procumbent form with an irregular spreading habit. Any vertical shoots that appear will have to be removed to maintain the shape. (4–6 ft; 1.2–1.8 m.)

A. *lasiocarpa*, another mountain species from North America of naturally slow growth, has given us an even slower-growing form in 'Compacta'. This is a broadly conical bush of irregular outline with attractive greyish green foliage. (Ultimately 6 ft; 1.8 m.)

A. *nordmanniana* has given rise to a delightful golden dwarf form, 'Golden Spreader', a rarity among the firs. The short prostrate branches bear bright golden yellow foliage whose colour intensifies during the winter. It is best grown in semi-shade to prevent scorching by the sun. ($1 \times 1\frac{1}{2}$ ft; 30×50 cm.)

A. *procera*, aptly called the noble fir, is a native of western North America and has branches densely furnished with greyish green foliage. It will not grow well on chalk soils. A fine dwarf from is 'Glauca Prostrata', which probably originated as a side graft of the glaucous form and has bluish grey foliage. Slow-growing and of low spreading habit, it may sometimes produce vertical shoots and these should be removed before they become too dominant. ($1 \times 3\frac{1}{4}$ ft; 30×100 cm.)

Above: foliage of *Abies*, left, and *Cedrus*, right.
Below: *Abies koreana*, naturally compact and slow-growing, produces its
beautiful cones at an early age (see p. 21)

Cedrus

The cedars are a magnificent group of conifers. They adorn many parks and large gardens with their elegance and grace, although they are often planted in spaces much too small for their extensive growth.

C. brevifolia is a typical mountain species, originating from Cyprus, and tends to be variable when raised from seed. With its small needles and slow growth, it has a dwarf appearance, which can be maintained by occasional careful pruning. (4 ft; 1.2 m.)

C. deodara, the Himalayan cedar, has the longest needles of all the species and a naturally drooping habit. There are several good forms, the most popular among the trees probably being 'Aurea'. For the smaller garden, however, the low-growing 'Aurea Nana'* is becoming better known.

'Golden Horizon'* is a recent introduction of semi-prostrate habit with gracefully weeping branches (2½–4 ft; 80–120 cm spread.)

'Nana'* forms a low bush and is very slow-growing. The compact branches will spread much wider than high, making this a very desirable dwarf conifer. (8 x 16 in.; 20 x 40 cm.)

'Pendula' could perhaps be more aptly named 'Prostrata', as it seems to prefer to hug the ground in a tumbling mass and can be quite vigorous in its spread. Timely removal of any ascending branches will maintain the creeping habit but, if a large weeping form is required, the leading shoot should be tied to a stake when young.

'Pygmy'* is extremely slow-growing, making less than a foot (30 cm) in height in ten years and forming a tiny mound. With its striking glaucous foliage, it is a choice but very rare plant.

C. libani, the Lebanese cedar, is probably the most familiar of the cedars with its horizontal branching system and dark foliage.

'Comte de Dijon' is a very popular smaller form. It slowly becomes a dense conical bush, with branches held horizontally, and in time will grow into a substantial shrub. (3¼ ft; 1 m.)

Selected dwarf forms have occasionally appeared in seed beds of *C. libani* and have been given the epithet 'Nana'. Inevitably, these will differ in some respect from each other, but they will be similar in their bushy compact habit and slow growth and are worth including in a collection.

'Sargentii' is a distinct and valuable dwarf form which, when left to sprawl over a bank or wall, shows to advantage its long

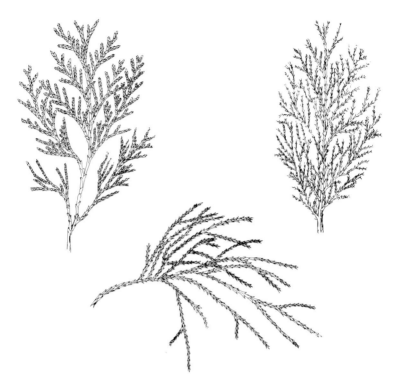

Foliage of *Chamaecyparis*: adult, left; juvenile, right; threadleaf, centre

pendulous branches. It can also be trained upwards to the height required and then allowed to display its weeping habit. (3¼ ft; 1 m.)

Chamaecyparis

This genus rates as probably the most prolific in cultivars suitable for the smaller garden. These have arisen usually as seedling variants or less often as branch sports. Of the five species hardy in Britain, three come from North America and two from Japan.

C. lawsoniana, Lawson's cypress, is well known for its usefulness as a hedging plant. It has produced a large number of extremely variable forms, from the taller-growing coloured kinds to the very dwarf ones, with many different types of foliage and shape. Most are easy to grow, preferring a moist but well-drained soil and, in the case of the yellow forms, a position in full sun to maintain the colour.

For convenience, many of the dwarf forms can be divided into groups sharing similar characteristics:

Ellwoodii group
'Ellwoodii' is widely grown and, although often offered as a dwarf, it will gain considerable height after many years. It is unrivalled among the forms with juvenile foliage, and its blue-green colour deepens in winter to a glaucous blue. Several good dwarf sports have occurred on 'Ellwoodii'.

'Chilworth Silver', also blue but of dwarfer habit, forms a fairly wide, upright, densely furnished bush.

'Ellwood's Gold' is a very attractive addition with its gold-tipped foliage and becomes a small conical bush. (4 ft; 1.1 m; see cover.)

'Ellwood's Pillar' is a miniature 'Ellwoodii' and makes a dense blue column suitable for a rock garden. (2 ft; 60 cm.)

'Ellwood's Pygmy', which is even lower-growing, is equally at home in the rock garden. It forms a rounded bun with similar blue colouring. (8 in.; 20 cm.)

'Blue Nantais' is a slow-growing conical plant of silvery blue. (3¼ ft; 1 m.)

Minima group
'Minima', like the other forms in this group, has normal adult foliage. It is a neatly compact plant which becomes a green globose bush (2 × 2 ft; 60 × 60 cm.)

'Minima Glauca' is of the same habit and growth rate, with a bluish grey tinge to the darker foliage.

'Minima Aurea', the golden form in this group, is slightly slower in growth. Its bright colour remains constant throughout the year. (2½ ft; 80 cm.)

'Aurea Densa' is almost indistinguishable from 'Minima Aurea' when young, although it will eventually produce a more conical shape and is densely furnished with stiff foliage held more tightly to the plant.

'Nana' is very similar to 'Minima' but will develop a more pointed top owing to the dominant central stem, whereas the 'Minima' forms have all the branches originating from a basal stub. The foliage is held slightly more loosely than in 'Minima' and the growth rate is faster. (2½ ft; 80 cm.)

'Nana Glauca' is the glaucous version with blue-green foliage.

'Gimbornii' has been a favourite for many years and, although similar to 'Nana Glauca', it is more globose in shape, denser in habit and very neat in outline.

'Gnome' forms a globe-shaped plant of deep green with small closely held foliage. It often produces coarser growth, which should be pinched out at an early stage, otherwise it will take over and spoil the tight habit. It is ideal for the rock garden or small border. (1 ft; 30 cm.)

'Green Globe'* is a real miniature and one of the most compact forms, slowly becoming a tight congested bun. It is perfect for the small rock garden or even a large trough and is a seedling introduction from New Zealand. (8–12 in.; 20–30 cm.)

'Pygmaea Argentea', a popular dwarf, is prettily variegated with silver on the tops of the foliage sprays and needs to be grown in full sun to keep the variegation sharp. It is sometimes damaged by winter weather, but soon recovers in the next growing season. ($3\frac{1}{4}$ ft; 1 m.)

Tamariscifolia group

'Tamariscifolia' belongs to a group of wide-spreading plants that do not form leaders and are consequently flat-topped. It has drooping sprays of light bluish green foliage. The habit is rather untidy in its young state, but eventually becomes more rounded, particularly if grown in a fully exposed situation. (2×4 ft; 60–120 cm.)

'Nestoides' is similar and very slow-growing, but not quite as wide-spreading.

'Nidiformis' is a very graceful cultivar, with horizontally held branches which gradually form a depression in the centre resembling a bird's nest. Its grey-green foliage has a glaucous bloom underneath. If grown in semi-shade, it will tend to be drawn upwards and lose its low-growing shape. (See below.)

C. obtusa is a Japanese species with dense dark green foliage which is distinctly blunt-ended and carried in flat sprays. It gives

Chamaecyparis lawsoniana 'Nidiformis' is distinguished from the very similar 'Tamariscifolia' by the bluntly rounded sprays of foliage

us an exciting range of dwarf conifers, a large number of which are exceptionally good for troughs and small rock gardens. So highly are they esteemed that many enthusiasts collect only *C. obtusa* cultivars.

Most of the smaller forms require protection in winter from the effects of freezing moisture, which can spoil their compact shape. Failing overhead protection in the garden, the best alternative is to grow them in pots and move them into a greenhouse or cold frame for the winter.

'Caespitosa'* is a tiny plant and much sought after. It forms a dense irregular bun with small shell-shaped sprays of foliage held tightly together and is very slow growing (4 in.; 10 cm.)

'Intermedia' grows a little faster and develops into a more pyramidal plant with slightly looser foliage. (6 in.; 15 cm.)

'Juniperoides' makes a rich green globose little plant, with the foliage held in open fan-shaped sprays. (6 in.; 15 cm.)

'Juniperoides Compacta'* is very similar in habit but more compact and closer-growing.

'Minima'* is a pygmy form with small tightly congested foliage resembling a pincushion. ($2\frac{1}{4} \times 4$ in.; 6×10 cm.)

'Nana' has upward-facing fans of foliage which form a rounded dense bush of irregular outline (6–8 in.; 15–20 cm.)

'Nana Aurea' is much more vigorous than 'Nana', despite its name. The typical fan-shaped foliage is golden on the outside of the plant fading to a yellowish green on the inside. ($1\frac{1}{2}$ ft; 50 cm.)

'Pygmaea' is a distinct flat-topped cultivar, with spreading branches of loose foliage and conspicuous brown stems. ($1\frac{1}{4} \times 2\frac{1}{4}$ ft; 45×70 cm.)

'Pygmaea Aurescens' is even more attractive than 'Pygmaea' turning to a rich bronze colour during the winter.

'Repens' is a prostrate form with short closely held sprays of bright green. It tends to send up vertical shoots which should be pruned occasionally to keep it low. (1×2 ft; 30×60 cm.)

'Rigid Dwarf', also listed as 'Rigida' or 'Nana Rigida' by some nurseries, is an upright plant of very dark green, tight, fan-shaped foliage borne vertically. The greyish bloom on the undersides of the leaves is a distinctive feature. (1 ft; 30 cm; see p. 15.)

'Filicoides', a distinctive form with fern-like foliage, may in time grow into an upright small tree of 5 feet (1.5 m). However, careful removal of the strongest shoots will keep it within bounds as a slow-growing shrubby bush.

'Compact Fernspray' is very similar (and sometimes offered as 'Filicoides Compacta'), although the fern-like branchlets are much smaller and make a low broadly bushy plant.

'Fernspray Gold' is a fairly recent introduction from New

Zealand. A beautiful golden yellow plant, its foliage is like 'Fili-coides' and carried on slightly arching branches. (Ultimately 5 ft; 1.5 m; see opposite.)

'Chabo-Yadori', unlike the species itself, has mostly juvenile foliage, with a crisped look to the branchlets caused by a few tips of adult foliage in irregular sprays. It is an upright small bush of light green (2 ft; 60 cm.)

'Mariesii' is a very pretty dwarf splashed with yellowish white on the tips of the foliage and of loose open habit. (2 ft; 60 cm.)

'Spiralis', with its twisted sprays of foliage, has a distinctive appearance and is an excellent cultivar of upright shape and slow growth. (10 in.; 25 cm.)

'Tonia' is a prettily variegated form which arose as a sport on 'Nana Gracilis'. The white splashes occur haphazardly over the plant and it should be grown in full sun for these to develop. (1¼ ft; 40 cm.)

'Nana Gracilis' is widely available from nurseries and, although it will eventually make a substantial bush, it is not too small for planting in a border. The dark green foliage is fairly loosely held in shell-shaped sprays. (4 ft; 1.2 m.)

C. *pisifera* is another Japanese species, with scale-like foliage which is rather prickly to the touch. It too has given rise to many dwarf cultivars of different foliage types. Apart from the forms with normal adult foliage, these may be divided into the Filifera group, which has whipcord type branchlets; the Plumosa group, which is softer than the adult type and is intermediate between that and the next group; and the Squarrosa group, which is a semi-juvenile type and fluffier in appearance.

Normal foliage group

'Compacta', bun-shaped with wholly adult foliage of a blue-green colour in close tight sprays, is an ideal rockery plant. (1½ × 2 ft; 20 × 30 cm.)

'Compacta Variegata' is irregularly splashed with creamy white patches and flecks and is slightly looser in habit than its green counterpart. (Eventually 2 × 5 ft; 60 × 150 cm.)

'Nana' is a choice bun-shaped dwarf of dark green with a whitish bloom on the undersides of the small adult foliage. (8 × 20 in.; 20 × 50 cm.)

'Nana Aureovariegata' has more of a golden lustre all over the plant than a definite variegation and is at its best in full sun. It is a compact form which hugs the contours of the ground, increasing very slowly in width to 1 foot (30 cm) or more.

Above: *Chamaecyparis obtusa* 'Fernspray Gold', a lovely golden version of 'Filicoides'

Below: *Chamaecyparis pisifera* 'Filifera Aureovariegata' is a striking plant for a sunny situation (see p. 30)

Filifera group

'Filifera Aurea' is a golden version of the threadleaf foliage type. Low and rounded at first, it becomes a vigorous erect plant of narrow branchlets which hang gracefully downwards and is very effective in a border. (3¼ ft; 1m.)

'Filifera Aureovariegata' is a delightful form with splashes of creamy white variegation. Like others in this group, it makes a mound of weeping thread-like foliage and needs full sun to bring out the variegation. (5 ft; 1.5 m; see p. 29.)

'Filifera Nana' is an all green compact plant of low broad habit. The narrow pendulous branches look well when allowed to drape over a wall or large rock. (1 × 3¼ ft; 30 × 100 cm.)

'Sungold', a recent introduction in the Filifera group, is also golden yellow and forms a dense globose bush. (2 ft; 60 cm.)

Plumosa group

'Plumosa Aurea Compacta' is a golden form and globose in habit. Although slow-growing, it may eventually reach 5 feet (1.5 m).

'Plumosa Compressa' is the smallest of the C. pisifera forms and perfect for the small rock garden with its tiny foliage packed into a round ball. The yellowish green colouring is brighter in summer. It may occasionally produce shoots of looser foliage, which should be removed. (8 in.; 20 cm.)

'Snow' is a low bun of soft moss-like foliage which is tipped with white. It needs to be positioned with some care in the garden, for the tips will burn if exposed to full sun and cold winds, while the branches will become long and drawn in heavy shade, spoiling the compact shape. A sheltered spot in semi-shade should keep it happy. (3¼ ft; 1 m.)

Squarrosa group

'Boulevard' has outstanding silver-blue Squarrosa-type foliage and makes a neat dense pyramid. It is always a popular choice. (3¼–5 ft; 1–1.5 m; see p. 6.)

'Squarrosa Intermedia' is the most attractive of the forms in the Squarrosa group, many of which can become quite large. It has typical, but smaller, blue-grey foliage and makes a rounded bush of tightly congested leaves. Any extra-long thin shoots should be pinched out to keep the plant dense and small. (1½ ft; 50 cm.)

C. thyoides, the white cypress from western North America, bears open sprays of glaucous green foliage. In its native land it grows happily on quite wet ground, but it dislikes shallow soils over chalk.

'Andelyensis' is a compact form with mostly adult foliage,

showing some juvenile foliage on the lower part of the plant. (5–6½ ft; 1.5–2 m.)

'Andelyensis Nana' an even smaller version, forms an upright bush with a flattish top and dense, dark bluish green foliage. (3¼ ft; 1 m.)

'Rubicon'* is a little conical bush of neat compact habit, with juvenile foliage which is green in summer, turning to plum purple in winter. Fairly new in cultivation, it is a choice plant for the rock garden. (2 ft; 60 cm.)

Cryptomeria

C. japonica is the sole species in this genus and a very important timber tree in its native Japan. It has given rise to many named forms, mostly of Japanese origin, both large and small and sometimes with unusual foliage.

'Bandai-Sugi' is a well-known cultivar, slow-growing and full of character. As well as the long shoots of small dark green foliage, there are areas of miniature tightly congested leaves which give the plant its irregular and rugged outline. (3¼ ft; 1 m.)

'Globosa Nana' is a lovely globe-shaped form of dense habit and rich green colouring. It has normal adult foliage, with the needles spirally arranged on long drooping shoots. (3¼–5 ft; 1–1.5 m; see p. 32.)

'Kilmacurragh' makes a low, flatly globose plant, unlike the many forms with abnormal foliage which are usually quite tall. The juvenile foliage with fasciated branch tips like cockscombs is a distinctive feature. (2–3 ft; 60–75 cm.)

'Elegans Compacta', although not exactly dwarf, is a distinct cultivar, with the soft juvenile foliage presenting a mass of billowing pale green. Reasonably slow-growing, it can develop into a compact, flat-topped, upright plant of 5 ft (1.5 m).

'Lobbii Nana' bears juvenile foliage as in 'Elegans Compacta' but, since the leaves are much stiffer and shorter, it forms a denser rounded bush. With age it develops clusters of congested foliage at the tips, the whole plant turning a purplish brown in winter. (2 ft; 60 cm.)

'Vilmoriniana' is a true dwarf of dense globose habit and one of the most popular forms for rock gardens. It changes to a purplish brown in winter. (1¼ × 1¼ ft; 40 × 40 cm.)

'Jindai Sugi', another popular cultivar, is a compact dense bush of soft green which retains its colour throughout the year. Short stiff needles borne on branches both erect and slightly spreading give it a more open and regular habit than 'Bandai-Sugi'. (4 ft; 1.2 m.)

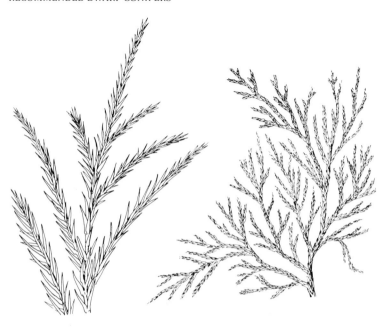

Above: foliage of *Cryptomeria*, left, and *Cupressus*, right
Below: with its pendulous branchlets, *Cryptomeria japonica* 'Globosa Nana' makes a graceful specimen for a low wall or lawn (see p. 31)

Two more compact and dense forms of the same foliage type are 'Nana' and 'Pygmaea'. Both are almost identical in their rounded shape, except that 'Nana' remains green all year while 'Pygmaea' turns a reddish bronze in winter. (2 ft; 60 cm.)

Cupressus

There are many species of true cypress, but very few are hardy enough to be grown outside in the British Isles and even these generally fare better in the south and west than in the north.

C. glabra is a tall pyramidal tree of glaucous foliage from Arizona. Probably the only truly dwarf form is 'Compacta'*, which is an excellent broadly conical bush of tightly congested grey-green foliage. ($1\frac{1}{2}$ ft; 45 cm.)

C. macrocarpa is well known for its fine golden forms which, given a mild sheltered spot, will make quite large trees relatively quickly. There are two very dwarf forms with green foliage worth looking for.
'Minima'*, with mainly juvenile foliage, forms a low, dense, rounded bush. Some longer adult branches may be produced, which should be removed. ($1\frac{1}{2}$–2 ft; 45–60 cm.)
'Pygmaea'* is a miniature selection which arose as a seedling and is a rare and choice plant. The tightly compressed bun-shaped plant will make little more than $1\frac{1}{2}$ feet (45 cm).

C. sempervirens, the Italian cypress, with its tall, dark green, narrow columns, is a familiar sight in the Mediterranean landscape, but only succeeds in the mildest areas of Britain.
'Swane's Golden' is a particularly good, slow-growing, golden form which develops into a slender compact column. Where it is happy it may well exceed 4 feet (1.2 m) after ten years.

Juniperus

This is a large genus with a wide geographical distribution and has greatly contributed to the enhancement of gardens with its many species, forms and cultivars. Junipers are generally very hardy, coming from areas of poor soil and rigorous climate, and will thrive in hot dry situations as well as tolerating chalk soils. They vary considerably in shape, from tall, broad or narrow columns to low ground-hugging types, and also in texture, size, habit and colour. Indeed, the harsh exposed conditions of the mountainside have given rise to a large number of prostrate forms, particularly in J. communis. A distinctive feature of the junipers is the production of berry-like fruits and not cones.

J. communis is one of the three British native conifers and is found throughout the northern hemisphere. The dense prickly foliage makes ideal ground cover and there are a large number of named forms.

'Compressa', everyone's ideal miniature for a trough or rock garden, is a tight grey-green column and will attain only 2 feet (60 cm) after many years. (See below.)

'Depressa Aurea' is a lovely spreading form with horizontal branches lifting slightly above the ground. The new growth in spring is a pretty yellow, changing in autumn to bronze with silvery bands on the undersides of the leaves. Planting in full sun will enhance the golden colour. (4 ft; 1.2 m spread; see opposite.)

Juniperus communis 'Compressa' is well known but susceptible to damage from wind and frost

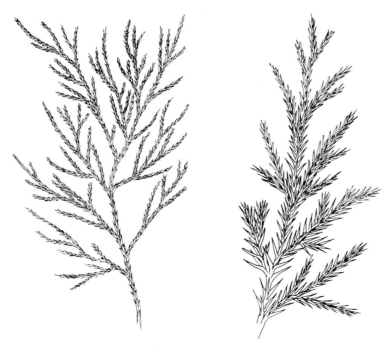

Above: foliage of *Juniperus*: adult, left; juvenile, right
Below: *Juniperus communis* 'Depressa Aurea' turns a beautiful bright
yellow in early summer

'Depressed Star' is a green form, with branches held closer to the ground. (4 ft; 1.2 m spread.)

'Hornibrookii' is a well-established cultivar among the ground-hugging forms. The branches lie flat and the short prickly leaves are twisted to display the white bands on top, giving the plant a silvery green appearance. (4 ft; 1.2 m spread; see p. 11.)

'Minima' is very similar to 'Hornibrookii' but with more obvious silvery bands on the larger leaves. It looks very effective trailing over rocks or a wall. (5 ft; 1.5 m.)

'Repanda' eventually becomes a low mound with dark green foliage which is soft to the touch. The radial growth from the centre of the plant results in a neat, almost circular outline and provides excellent ground cover where space is available.

Some more recent introductions of prostrate forms of *J. communis* are worth searching for, although they may not be readily available.

'Berkshire'* from North America, is slow-growing and cushion-like, which makes it suitable for more restricted areas.

'Gew Graze'*, a selection discovered in Cornwall, is similar to 'Repanda' but of slower growth and not quite so prostrate.

'Derrynane'*, an Award of Merit plant, deserves to be better known. It originally occurred in County Kerry and is a very prostrate form which produces berries freely.

J. conferta grows on sand dunes on the coasts of Japan, where the maritime exposure keeps it low and mat-forming. The sharply pointed green leaves make a dense carpet of some vigour.

Two forms introduced from North America are 'Blue Pacific'*, with a more procumbent habit and attractive blue-green needles; and 'Emerald Sea'*, a bright green colour forming a dense low mat. Both will have an eventual spread of 5 feet (1.5 m).

J. horizontalis, from North America, is probably the best species for ground cover. The many named forms come in a range of colours from grey-green to steel-blue, some of which take on a bronze hue for the winter. Most will cover an area of 3 feet (90 cm) quite rapidly, if fairly slowly at first, and occasional snipping back of the leading shoots in the early years will encourage dense growth from the main stems.

'Bar Harbor' is a thick mat of long, thin branches, greyish green turning to a mauve-purple in the winter. The colour is most pronounced when the plant is grown in full sun.

'Douglasii' is similar but more greyish in colour as the foliage is covered with a glaucous bloom. It also becomes purplish in winter.

'Emerald Spreader', a newcomer to the trade, should become very popular for its bright green foliage and dense growth.

'Glauca' is steel-blue, very prostrate and with long thin branchlets which tend to overlap in layers.

'Glomerata'* is distinctive for its short vertical shoots of dense rich green foliage. The prostrate main stems cover the ground less rapidly than in other forms.

'Grey Pearl', unlike most cultivars of *J. horizontalis*, is a dumpy little blue-green plant of wholly erect branches, which gradually becomes wider than it is high. (8–12 in.; 20–30 cm.)

'Plumosa Compacta' represents a group of forms characterized by the branches being held at an ascending angle radiating from the centre. It eventually makes a rather flat-topped thick bush and the light grey-green foliage turns purplish bronze in winter.

J. × media is the group name for hybrids between *J. chinensis* and *J. sabina*. The commonest is 'Pfitzeriana', which has great architectural value. Its wide-spreading branches are capable of covering a large area. Although most of the hybrids are too big for the small garden, there are a few that would be appropriate.

'Pfitzeriana Compacta' is a slow-growing version and forms a flat-topped compact plant with prickly foliage. ($3\frac{1}{4} \times 6\frac{1}{2}$ ft; 1×2 m.)

'Gold Coast' is a lovely golden form, also of low bushy habit. It is an outstanding cultivar with horizontally held branches. (3×4 ft; 90×120 cm.)

'Old Gold' appeared as a sport on the vigorous *J. × media* 'Pfitzeriana Aurea', but it is more compact and slower-growing. The golden colour persists all through the plant. It is larger than 'Gold Coast', with wider-spreading branches.

J. 'Grey Owl' should be mentioned here. Previously classified under *J. virginiana* and occasionally under *J. sabina*, it has now been established that it is a hybrid between *J. × media* 'Pfitzeriana', which gives it the low spreading habit, and *J. virginiana* 'Glauca', which provides the glaucous blue colour. It is an exceptional cultivar, ultimately a large wide-spreading shrub but slow growing. (2×5 ft; 60×150 cm.)

'Blaauw' belongs to the Plumosa group, which is quite different, with tightly congested foliage on branches growing at a more upright angle. It is blue-green and the leaves are densely held on short side branches. (4 ft; 1.2 m.)

'Globosa Cinerea' is almost identical to 'Blaauw' when young, but slightly less tall and becoming much broader with age.

'Shimpaku'*, the smallest member of the group, is much used for bonsai. Soft grey-green foliage makes a compact miniature version of the Plumosa type. (1 ft; 30 cm.)

J. procumbens is a prostrate mountain species from Japan of quite vigorous habit, sending out long branches of small greyish green leaves. (Ultimate spread 6½ ft; 2 m.)

'Nana' is a very reliable, more compact form of bright green prickly foliage. With its completely flat dense habit, it is excellent for suppressing weeds. This distinctive cultivar is a favourite with collectors. (Ultimate spread 4 ft; 1.2 m.)

J. recurva, the drooping juniper of the Himalayas, has a graceful, botanical variety in var. *coxii*. Eventually a large tree, but slow-growing in cultivation, this has rich green foliage held tightly to the thin branchlets and a delightful weeping habit.

'Densa'* has smaller foliage than var. *coxii* and is low-growing and compact. The spreading semi-prostrate branches nod gently at the tips and it will do best in full sun. (1¼ × 2 ft; 40–60 cm.)

J. rigida, the needle juniper, is very prickly indeed and normally a tallish shrub with drooping tips. However, 'Prostrata'* is, as the name suggests, a low-growing plant of dense habit with yellowish brown branchlets.

J. sabina, the savin juniper, and its forms are mainly low-growing shrubs of spreading habit. 'Tamariscifolia' is by far the best and quickly makes a mat of dark green foliage, which is useful for covering unsightly areas (1 × 4 ft; 30 × 120 cm.)

J. scopulorum, a species from the mountains of western North America, has given rise to many named forms, the majority of them narrow pyramids of silver-grey. 'Repens' is one of the prostrate forms, with long brown stems and bluish green foliage. It is slow-growing and spreads to 4 feet (1.2 m).

J. squamata has produced two selections of an outstanding blue. They provide a striking contrast when planted among green and gold conifers.

'Blue Carpet', a semi-prostrate form of intense blue, is thickly furnished with prickly foliage and will spread to about 5 feet (1.5 m). Any rising branches should be removed when they appear to keep it low.

'Blue Star' is one of the best dwarf conifers and therefore relatively easy to obtain. A sturdy little plant of irregular outline, it makes a compact bush. (1¼ × 1½ ft; 40 × 50 cm; see opposite.)

'Glassell'*, with short grey-green leaves similar to those of *J. recurva*, is very slow-growing. The near vertical branches have

The very slow-growing *Juniperus squamata* 'Blue Star' remains dense and low

short side branchlets which curve gently downwards, forming an attractive dense little bush.

'Loderi', a well-known cultivar, is a low column of blue-green colour. The short needles are densely arranged on upright branches. ($3\frac{1}{4}$–5 ft; 1–1.5 m.)

'Pygmaea'* is one of the smallest forms of the species, with grey-green leaves. A stocky little plant, it is very similar to 'Glassell' but without the curving branchlets. ($3\frac{1}{4} \times 3\frac{1}{4}$ ft; 1×1 m.)

J. virginiana, another North American species, is represented by many named forms, most of which grow too tall for inclusion here. There are a few exceptions.

'Blue Cloud' is compact and slow-growing with bright blue-grey foliage. Although very dense in the centre, it has long slightly twisted branches which give it a distinctive appearance. ($1\frac{1}{2} \times 5$ ft; 50×150 cm.)

39

'Globosa'* is a rich green, globose, compact bun, rather irregular in shape when young, becoming more symmetrical later. (2½ × 2½ ft; 80 × 80 cm.)

'Pendula Nana'* is a collector's item and much sought after, but difficult to obtain owing to its singularly slow growth. The long, thin, greyish green branches grow horizontally unless encouraged to form a main stem to about 1 foot (30 cm) and then allowed to droop. It needs protection from winter weather.

Larix

The larches are unusual among conifers in that they shed their leaves for the winter. Most people will be familiar with the striking golden yellow colour of *Larix decidua* in a woodland in autumn. In spring too the trees look most attractive as the buds burst open to reveal fresh, bright green, new leaves.

L. decidua, the European larch, has a particularly fine dwarf form called 'Corley'* which, although not readily available, is certainly worth seeking out. It forms a low rounded bush of slow growth. (2 × 3¼ ft; 60 × 100 cm.)

L. kaempferi, the Japanese larch, is a beautiful species with red-brown bark and twigs. There are two dwarf forms of note.

'Nana'* is typical of a witch's broom with its dense compact habit and makes a very dwarf globose bush. (1½ ft; 50 cm.)

'Varley'* has a slower annual growth rate, but its longer leaves give it a very dense habit.

Picea

In their natural state the spruces are highly ornamental trees, generally of narrow pyramidal outline, and of course much too large for most gardens. They thrive in moist but well-drained soil and in long spells of dry weather they benefit from being sprayed with water, which helps to prevent attacks by mites and subsequent loss of the leaves.

P. abies, the well-known Norway spruce, is much used in forestry and especially for the production of Christmas trees. The numerous dwarf and slow-growing forms of this species are popular for rock gardens or as specimen plants, ranging from the tall strong varieties to the low-growing and very dwarf.

'Clanbrassiliana' eventually becomes a small conical bush. With its short rigid branches, it is dense and compact and has a very slow rate of growth. (3¼ ft; 1 m.)

Above: foliage of *Larix*, left, and *Picea*, right.
Below: 'Gregoryana', one of the best dwarf forms of *Picea abies*, was introduced in the 1850s (see p. 42)

'Elegans' was one of the earliest forms to be named. Short branches and small leaves make this an extremely compact plant and the reddish brown buds contrast pleasantly with the light green leaves.

'Gregoryana' is a most distinctive cultivar with its prickly leaves of light green. A low dense cushion, it becomes more irregular in outline with age. (6 × 8 in.; 15 × 20 cm; see p. 41.)

'Little Gem' is a diminutive plant, forming a tight little bun with very small leaves and branches.

'Nidiformis' has been well known for many years. Its spreading branches make a flat-topped plant of uniform shape. ($1\frac{1}{4}$ × 2 ft; 40 × 60 cm.)

'Procumbens' is low and spreading, with branches held in layers and tips rising slightly. (1 × $6\frac{1}{2}$ ft; 30 × 200 cm; see opposite.)

'Pygmaea', an old favourite and very slow-growing, is a compact conical bush. It tends to produce branches of normal growth which vary in vigour and must be removed. ($1\frac{1}{2}$ ft; 50 cm.)

P. glauca, the white spruce of Canada, has foliage of dark glaucous green and has given us the most consistently popular dwarf form in 'Albertiana Conica'. This is a first-class garden plant of conical shape and neat compact habit. ($2\frac{1}{2}$ ft; 80 cm.)

'Alberta Globe' is a branch sport of 'Albertiana Conica', recently introduced, and forms a low neat mound. It is much in demand as a rock garden plant. ($1\frac{1}{2}$ ft; 50 cm.)

'Laurin'* is identical to 'Albertiana Conica', but smaller in all its parts. (10 in.; 25 cm.)

P. mariana has given rise to the attractive blue-grey 'Nana', which is the most popular dwarf form of this species. It is a neat little rounded bush with branches regularly arranged from the centre. ($1\frac{1}{2}$ × $3\frac{1}{4}$ ft; 50 × 100 cm.)

P. omorika, the Serbian spruce, is a graceful slender tree and, in its native habitat on limestone slopes in Yugoslavia, it is an impressive sight. The bicoloured leaves of green above and greyish blue below are a pleasing attribute.

'Nana' is an excellent dwarf form in which the foliage colour combination is very noticeable. Eventually pyramidal in shape, this lovely compact plant will reach 4 feet (1.2 m.)

P. × mariorika, is a hybrid of P. mariana and P. omorika, which occurred in a European nursery and is intermediate between its parents. There are a few good dwarf selections.

Above: *Picea abies* 'Procumbens', a distinctive flat-topped plant with stiff, widespreading sprays of foliage

Below: 'Globosa', a superb dwarf form of the Colorado spruce, *Picea pungens* (see p. 44)

'Gnom', sometimes offered as *P. omorika* 'Gnom', is a dense conical plant with very sharply pointed needles, green above and whitish beneath. (2½ ft; 75 cm.)

'Kobold' is a more globose shape and the needles are dark green on the underside and whitish above. (2¼ × 5 ft; 75 × 150 cm.)

'Machala' has foliage which is bluish green and silvery and makes a wide-spreading, flatly globose plant. (About 1½ × 3¼ ft; 50 × 100 cm.)

P. orientalis, a tall handsome tree from the Caucasus mountains, is a neat densely branched pyramid with dark green needles which are shorter than those of *P. abies*. There are a few cultivars, most of which ultimately become quite tall.

'Gracilis', a slow-growing form with typically dense habit, starts as a round-topped bush. However, the new growth rises to produce a network of branches pointing in all directions and once a dominant leader has emerged, it becomes a more pyramidal small tree. (4 ft; 1.2 m.)

'Nana'* is a smaller version of 'Gracilis' and quite rare in cultivation. It has very dark green needles and is a globose to oval plant, usually not more than 3¼ feet (1 m) high.

P. pungens, the Colorado spruce, has an exceptional range of forms with intense blue foliage. Many of the named cultivars, although slow-growing, eventually develop into large shrubs and are ideal specimens or spot plants for the lawn.

'Globosa' is a true dwarf, whose silvery blue leaves are smaller than normal. The closely arranged branches form a thick bushy plant which is excellent for the smaller garden. (2 × 2 ft; 60 × 60 cm; see p. 43.)

'Glauca Prostrata' and other procumbent varieties are usually the result of propagating from side branches and, because these shoots are weaker, they prefer to hug the ground. This slow-growing, semi-prostrate cultivar gives a striking display of bright blue foliage, particularly when draping a wall or bank with its irregular growth.

Pinus

The pines are probably the most easily recognized group of conifers and include many large attractive trees, as well as others from mountainous regions suitable for small gardens. The numerous different species cover a wide geographical area, distributed throughout the northern hemisphere from the Arctic Circle down to the Equator. Pines are well suited to poor drier

Foliage of *Pinus*: 2 leaves, left; 3 leaves, right; 5 leaves, centre

conditions and are less demanding than other conifers. The narrow needles are held in either twos, threes or fives, according to species, and vary in length. The genus is represented by many ornamental forms of great garden value.

P. aristata is a natural slow grower, owing to the influence of the dry mountain conditions of its native home of southwestern North America, and some specimens in the wild are believed to be the oldest living trees on earth. It has great character and grows into an attractive upright bush, thickly covered with grey-blue needles which are more bunched at the tips—whence the common names bristlecone and foxtail pine. It is easily distinguished by the droplets of resin on the needle tips. ($3\frac{1}{4}$ ft; 1 m.)

P. cembra, the Arolla pine from the mountains of central Europe and northern Asia, is a highly ornamental species of neat regular outline and broadly conical habit. The short bluish green needles are held in groups of five and densely clothe the stems. (Eventually $6\frac{1}{2}$ ft; 2 m.)

'Aureovariegata'* has yellowish needles, the colour being at its best in winter, and is slower growing.

(Some nurseries may offer cultivars with the names 'Globe' and 'Pygmaea', but these have now been assigned to *P. pumila*. See p. 50).

P. contorta, the lodgepole pine, is a relatively small species from North America and varies according to its location from a contorted shrub to a tall columnar tree. One particularly good dwarf form which should become popular is 'Spaan's Dwarf'*, an open low bush with pairs of short mid-green needles closely set on the upright branches. ($2\frac{1}{2}$ ft; 75 cm.)

P. densiflora is much used in its native Japan for landscape planting, because of its irregular growth pattern and adaptability to pruning. There are a number of named cultivars, a few of which make good dwarf trees.

'Alice Verkade' is an attractive dome-shaped plant with typically long bright green needles held in pairs. ($3\frac{1}{4}$ ft; 1 m.)

'Globosa' is a low and rounded plant, with shorter needles than usual and a very dense habit. (See p. 48.)

'Umbraculifera', which means 'umbrella-like', is an apt name for this slow-growing form with upright and spreading branches and dense dark green needles. ($3\frac{1}{4} \times 3\frac{1}{4}$ ft; 1×1 m.)

P. leucodermis, a strong-growing species from the Balkan

mountains, has characteristically dense and rigid dark green needles. It is sometimes to be found under the name P. *heldreichii* var. *leucodermis*.

'Compact Gem' makes a lovely specimen plant. Initially a low rounded bush, it becomes more pyramidal as the main stems increase in height. (4 × 3 ft; 120 × 90 cm.)

'Schmidtii'* may be offered under the name 'Pygmy' but is very rare. It becomes a tight small dome of dark green rigid foliage and is ideal for growing in a pot. (See p. 48.)

P. *mugo*, the mountain pine, is a very variable species in the wild and ranges from a low dwarf to a small shrubby tree. Unnamed plants in a nursery may turn out to be more vigorous than they seem and it is wise to bear this in mind when deciding on their position in the garden. There are a number of excellent named forms and most are easily obtainable.

'Corley's Mat'* is reliably prostrate, forming a mat of dark green leaves not more than 1 foot (30 cm) high and about 3 feet (90 cm) spread. (See p. 49.)

'Gnom', from Holland, is probably one of the best known selections. It is a compact little bush of 2½ feet (80 cm).

'Mops' is very similar, but a little lower and wider and consequently more bun-shaped.

P. *parviflora*, the Japanese white pine, is a superb small species in its own right and a great favourite for bonsai in its native land. The fine blue-grey needles are held in clusters of five and it has a pleasing irregular outline and very slow growth. The species itself is well worth giving garden room and there are also several cultivars.

'Adcock's Dwarf'*, selected in Britain, is a dense bush of extremely slow growth and rather irregular outline. It has short greyish needles more clustered at the tips of the slender stems. (1½ ft; 50 cm.)

'Negishi', a Japanese name meaning short-needled, may be applied to several different selections. As a rule it makes a low, almost pyramidal, bush with irregular branching and small glaucous leaves.

'Brevifolia' is more upright and narrow in habit, with short, stiff, bluish green needles. (Eventually 4ft; 1.2 m.)

P. *pumila* is another Japanese pine, very similar to P. *cembra* but usually lower in habit and smaller in all its parts. It has comparatively short glaucous green leaves.

'Dwarf Blue'* is a choice plant of low, broad, bushy habit. The

Above: *Pinus densiflora* 'Globosa', a slow-growing hemispherical bush (see p. 46)

Below: the choice *Pinus leucodermis* 'Schmidtii', recorded as growing only 1½ ft (50 cm) in 40 years (see p. 47)

Above: 'Corley's Mat', a recently introduced ground-hugging form of
Pinus mugo (see p. 47)

Below: *Pinus pumila* 'Dwarf Blue', a desirable but uncommon
plant (see p. 47)

bundles of blue-grey needles with distinct white bands give it great attraction ($1\frac{1}{2}$ × 4 ft; 50 × 120 cm; see p. 49.)

'Globe' a globose bush of dense blue-grey colour, is becoming better known. It is very slow-growing, producing cones when quite young and red male flowers in the spring.

P. strobus, the Weymouth pine, is a large beautiful tree from North America. The long, thin, pale blue-green needles are carried in groups of five and it readily gives rise to variations from seed.

'Densa'* has shorter needles than normal, which are exceptionally thin. Still new to cultivation, it should maintain its compact, dense habit and remain low for many years.

'Nana', the most popular form, is so thickly covered with needles that the branches are completely hidden. It becomes a compact globe. ($2\frac{1}{2}$ × $3\frac{1}{4}$ ft; 75 × 100 cm.)

'Prostrata' needs space to develop and the procumbent branches of normal-sized foliage will in time make quite a large spreading plant.

P. sylvestris, the Scots pine, is the most familiar and recognizable conifer in the British Isles. It has a tendency to produce witch's brooms, which has led to the introduction of numerous dwarf selections from this source, in addition to many others of seedling origin.

'Beuvronensis' has been in the trade for a long time and is typical of the dense habit of a witch's broom. It makes a broad compact bush of grey-green and may require occasional pruning to maintain the density. ($2\frac{1}{2}$ × $3\frac{1}{4}$ ft; 75 × 100 cm.)

'Aurea' a distinct slow-growing form, has leaves of deep yellow in winter, turning to pale green in summer.

'Gold Coin' and 'Gold Medal' are two excellent coloured varieties, both light green in summer changing to an intense golden yellow in winter. They should be planted in full sun for the best display and are of upright compact habit. 'Gold Medal' will grow to about 2 feet (60 cm); 'Gold Coin' (opposite) will be taller.

'Doone Valley'*, a miniature which is perhaps the most compact of the dwarf forms, is perfect for the rock garden. It will eventually become a broad conical bush of irregular outline with blue-green needles. ($1\frac{1}{4}$ × 1 ft; 40 × 30 cm.)

'Globosa' sometimes known as 'Glauca Globosa', is low-growing and compact. It makes a small globose shrub, with the short grey-green needles held on stiff upright branches.

'Globosa Viridis', despite its name, is entirely different and has a dense, almost shaggy, appearance with its long, dark green,

Above: 'Gold Coin', a reliable dwarf variety of Pinus sylvestris with stronger colouring than 'Aurea'

Below: Pinus sylvestris 'Watereri', an upright form originally found on a Surrey common in the mid-nineteenth century (see p. 52)

slightly twisted needles. It starts as low and globose, becoming more oval in time. (About 3¼ft; 1 m.)

'Moseri' is a well-established cultivar similar to 'Globosa Viridis', distinguished from it by the fact that the long green needles turn an attractive yellow in winter.

'Nana' is a small bushy plant of very slow growth and blue-grey needles. (1½ ft; 50 cm.)

'Watereri', occasionally found under the name 'Pumila', is like 'Nana' but more vigorous. Although slow-growing, it will ultimately be quite a substantial small tree of broadly conical shape. (5 ft; 1.5 m; see p. 51.)

Pseudotsuga

P. menziesii, the Douglas fir of North America, has foliage very similar to Abies but narrower and softer. Of the few species in this genus, it is the one most commonly cultivated, both for timber and in gardens. Over the years a number of cultivars have been introduced, but only a few dwarf forms are now available from nurseries.

'Brevifolia' is an extremely slow-growing shrubby form to begin with, although eventually it becomes a small tree. The short, narrow, light green leaves are held densely around the branchlets. (2½ ft; 75 cm.)

'Densa'* is a dumpy little plant with a flat top and irregular habit, suitable for the rock garden. It has short dark green needles on twiggy, horizontally held branches. (Eventually 3¼ ft; 1 m.)

'Glauca' is a blue-leaved form and slower-growing than the species. A seedling from this named 'Fletcheri' is probably the most popular of the Douglas firs. A fine blue colour, it grows into a compact more or less rounded shrub of irregular outline and with a flat top. (2 ft; 60 cm.)

Taxus

The yews are a group of conifers of considerable garden merit. They are very hardy and tolerant of most types of soil and situation, being particularly useful in areas of heavy shade. Like the juniper, the seed of the yew is encased in a berry-like fruit which is normally red, although there is a yellow-fruited form of T. baccata.

T. baccata, the common English yew, has given us the most variation in form and colour.

'Adpressa Aurea', a gold form which is less vigorous than

Foliage of *Pseudotsuga*, left, and *Taxus*, right

'Adpressa', makes a dense spreading shrub. The small yellowish leaves are more golden in the spring when the new growth begins. (Eventually 5 ft; 1.5 m.)

'Amersfoort' is an unusual open-growing shrub, with small rounded leaves held on upright branches. (3¼ ft; 1 m.)

'Compacta', with normal dark green foliage, is a most attractive compact, conical bush of upright branches. (Ultimately 4 ft; 1.2 m.)

53

'Ericoides', a small upright bush, has small glossy green leaves held closely to the stems. (Eventually $3\frac{1}{4}$ft; 1 m.)

'Nutans' is a tiny, dense, dumpy bush, with a flat top and dark green leaves on short upright branches. (1 ft; 30 cm.)

'Repandens', low-growing and spreading, is particularly valuable for ground. cover in shade, and also does well. in sun. ($1\frac{1}{2}$–$6\frac{1}{2}$ ft; 50–200 cm.)

'Repens Aurea', another prostrate variety, has bright yellow variegated leaves. It will lose the variegation if grown in shade.

'Standishii', a very well known cultivar, is extremely slow-growing. It forms a small solid column of bright golden yellow. ($1\frac{1}{2}$ ft; 50 cm.)

'Summergold', a fairly recent introduction, has bright golden yellow foliage and is semi-prostrate. ($1\frac{1}{2} \times 3\frac{1}{4}$ ft; 50×100 cm.)

T. cuspidata, the Japanese yew, is very hardy and is often grown in colder areas where T. baccata will not survive. There are some good dwarf forms.

'Aurescens' is a charming low compact shrub whose new golden yellow shoots turn green later in the season. (1×3 ft; 30–90 cm.)

'Densa' is a broad and low plant of dense dark green leaves on short branches. ($1\frac{1}{2}$ ft; 50 cm.)

Thuja

The arborvitae are sometimes confused with the genus Chamaecyparis since they bear the same type of flattened foliage sprays. The most obvious difference is the shape of the cones, which are oblong on thujas and globular on Chamaecyparis, while the leaves of the thujas have a distinctively pungent smell when crushed. Like Chamaecyparis the thujas are also prolific in the production of dwarf forms.

T. occidentalis, an American species, has a number of good dwarf forms, mostly with normal adult foliage, a few with juvenile leaves.

'Caespitosa' is a small globose bun of compact habit and flattened adult foliage. ($1 \times 1\frac{1}{2}$ ft; 30×40 cm.)

'Ericoides', a fairly vigorous, juvenile-foliaged form, is a striking bronze colour in winter. ($3\frac{1}{4}$ ft; 1 m.)

'Filiformis' is a very distinct cultivar and has long thread-like branches of a rich green contrasting with the orange-brown stems. ($2\frac{1}{2}$ ft; 80 cm.)

Above: foliage of *Thuja*
Below: *Thuja occidentalis* 'Rheingold', indispensable for its golden
winter colour (see p. 56)

'Globosa', a widely grown variety of compact adult foliage, forms a neat symmetrical globe of light greyish green and keeps its colour throughout the year. (3¼ ft; 1 m.)

'Golden Globe' is an outstanding golden colour with a compact globose habit. (Ultimately 4ft; 1.2 m.)

'Little Gem' becomes a flattened mound of compact, rich green, adult foliage. It has a rather untidy habit with the branches held in a haphazard fasion. (1¼ ft; 40 cm.)

'Rheingold' is undoubtedly one of the best known conifers in gardens. Initially a rounded bun of rich gold, it gradually gains a more pyramidal shape. It is a beautiful colour and a useful plant for any garden, although there are various forms sold under this name which grow up to 10 feet (3 m) high. (2¼ ft; 70 cm; see p. 55.)

T. orientalis, from China, is easily distinguished from other thujas by the foliage. This is held in vertical sprays which look as if they have been slotted together. There are several excellent and reliable dwarf forms including some with juvenile foliage.

'Aurea Nana' is commonly grown and easily obtainable. A compact oval bush of deep yellow, it needs to be grown in full sun to keep its colour and dense habit. (3¼ ft; 1 m; see opposite.)

'Semperaurescens' is similar in habit and colour, but much more vigorous and it would soon outgrow its place in rock garden. So too would 'Elegantissima', which turns bronze in winter. Both are more appropriate for a border. (4 ft; 1.2 m.)

'Conspicua' is also a quick grower, more columnar in shape, and retains its golden colour through the winter. (See opposite.)

'Collen's Gold' and 'Golden Minaret' are two new golden introductions, both slow-growing. 'Collen's Gold' has an upright narrow habit, whereas 'Golden Minaret' forms a slender cone-shaped plant. (4 ft; 1.2 m.)

'Juniperoides', a juvenile-foliaged form, is outstanding for its plum colour in winter. In summer the soft foliage is green and it forms a dense rounded bush of about 3¼ feet (1 m).

'Rosedalis', another popular juvenile-foliaged form, is a neatly rounded and compact bush. Its particular attraction is the range of colours it assumes through the year, from the bright yellow of its spring growth to green in summer and then purplish in winter. (3¼ ft; 1 m.)

'Sieboldii' is the green counterpart of the yellow adult foliage forms. Very densely clothed with the usual vertical branches, it forms a round-topped bush and would have a rate of growth intermediate between 'Aurea Nana' and 'Semperaurescens'.

T. plicata, the western red cedar, comes from the forests of

Above: Conifer garden, *Thuja orientalis* 'Aurea Nana' (on left) with other dwarf and slow-growing varieties and heather underplanting

Below: among the golden forms of *Thuja orientalis*, 'Conspicua' is valuable for keeping its colour throughout the year

western North America. It is a large stately tree, important for the production of high-quality timber for the building trade. The aromatic foliage is similar to that of *Thuja occidentalis*. There are a few excellent dwarf forms, most of which are golden-leaved.

'Cuprea', a very slow-growing dwarf conical bush, is unlikely to exceed 2½ to 3¼ feet (75–100 cm). The compact bronze-yellow foliage sprays spread slightly at the tips.

'Rogersii' is similar in colouring, but makes a globose bush with denser foliage, green on the less exposed parts of the plant and golden bronze on the outside. It is probably the best known cultivar. (Ultimately 3¼ ft; 1 m; see opposite.)

'Stoneham Gold' also has a similar colour combination, the inner foliage being very dark green and the tips an attractive orange-yellow. It is very slow-growing, but in time will be taller than 'Cuprea' and 'Rogersii'.

'Hillieri', a familiar all-green cultivar, is a very dense rounded shrub. It tends to produce long thin shoots, which should be removed. (3¼ × 3¼ ft; 1 × 1 m.)

Tsuga

The hemlocks are a major feature of the landscape of North America. The foliage is like that of the yew with its flat blunt-ended needles, except that these are much finer and thinner.

T. canadensis, alone of the species, has given us a plethora of named forms, originating mainly from North America. Among them are some very fine dwarf cultivars.

'Cole' an extremely popular prostrate variety, was found in the wild. The branches press themselves tightly to the ground, the main ones becoming characteristically bare of leaves at the centre. However, it is possible to train the leading stem upwards for a few inches to encourage a weeping habit. (3¼ ft; 1 m.)

'Jeddeloh', a recent introduction from Europe, has semi-prostrate branches forming a flat-topped globose bush with a slightly depressed centre of light green foliage. (1¼ × 3¼ ft; 50 × 100 cm; see p. 60.)

'Jervis' is a true dwarf of exceptionally slow growth, with tightly compressed small foliage. The dense compacted branches give it an irregular chunky outline. (1 ft; 30 cm.)

Opposite: *Thuja plicata* 'Rogersii' produces strong vertical shoots which may be cut out to maintain a more compact shape

Above: foliage of *Tsuga*
Below: *Tsuga canadensis* 'Jeddeloh' originated as a selected seedling in a West German nursery (see p. 59)

Above: 'Pendula', a spectacular weeping form of *Tsuga canadensis* (see p. 62)

Below: conifers are a great feature in the Valley Gardens at Windsor Great Park

'Minima', contrary to its name, is low spreading and far from being the smallest form of the species. It is very attractive, with the branches rising at a low angle and gracefully drooping at the tips. Another cultivar named 'Bennett' is considered by some authorities to be synonymous. ($1 \times 2\frac{1}{2}$ ft; 30×75 cm.)

'Minuta'* is probably the dwarfest form in cultivation and certainly a plant to seek out. It is a diminutive bush of tightly congested branches and tiny leaves. (8 in.; 20 cm.)

'Pendula' is a slow-growing form that needs initial training of the main stem to the desired height for the weeping habit to be fully appreciated. If left to its own devices, it will become procumbent and spreading rather than pendulous. (See p. 61.)

Such a vast number of conifer cultivars have appeared in cultivation over a long period that it is impossible to do justice to them all and these descriptions can only scratch the surface. Although most good nurseries and garden centres offer the popular forms, it is the specialist nurseries that stock the rare and the unusual. They are well worth visiting to see the exciting range available.

The popular dwarf, *Chamaecyparis lawsoniana* 'Pygmaea Argenta', may be damaged by winter weather, but recovers in the next growing season

Index

Page numbers in **bold** refer to illustrations

63